CW00664861

# BRANCH LINE TO
# BUDE

## Vic Mitchell and Keith Smith

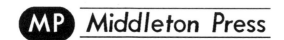

**MP** Middleton Press

*Cover picture: Okehampton footbridge frames the Bulleid designed coaches which form the 3.48pm from Exeter Central on 25th July 1961. The locomotive is class U1 no. 31903, built in 1931. (E.W.Fry)*

*First published May 1994*


*ISBN 1 873793 29 4*

*© Middleton Press 1994*

*Design - Deborah Goodridge*
*Typesetting -  Barbara Mitchell*
              *Deborah Goodridge*

*Published by Middleton Press*
              *Easebourne Lane*
              *Midhurst*
              *West Sussex*
              *GU29 9AZ*
              *Tel: (0730) 813169*
*(From 16 April 1995 - (01730) 813169)*

*Printed & bound by Biddles Ltd,*
              *Guildford and Kings Lynn*

# INDEX

# ACKNOWLEDGEMENTS

We are very grateful for the assistance received from so many of those mentioned in the credits and also from A.E.Bennett, N.L.Browne, R.M.Casserley, G.Croughton, J.N.Faulkner, Mrs S.Grove, M.King, A.Ll.Lambert, N.Langridge, T.Reardon, Mr D. & Dr. S.Salter, N.Sprinks, N.Stanyon, E.Wilmshurst, E.Youldon and our ever helpful wives.

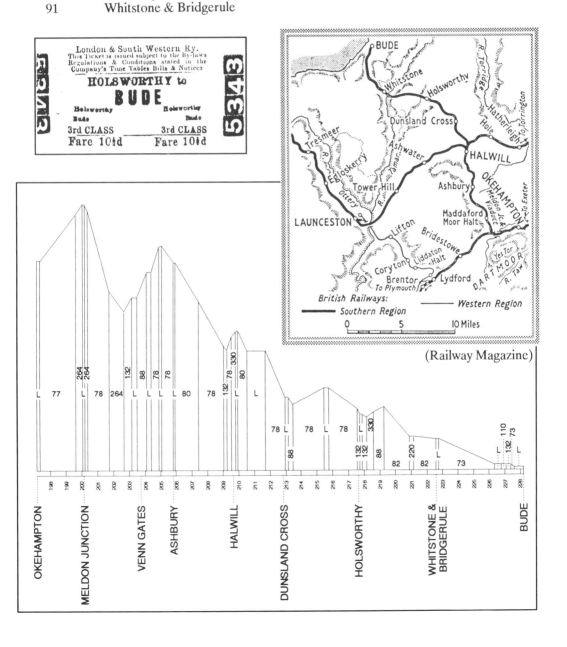

(Railway Magazine)

# GEOGRAPHICAL SETTING

The small market town of Okehampton is situated to the north of the highest part of Dartmoor at about 500ft above sea level. The line climbs for three miles at mostly 1 in 77 to Meldon Junction. The nearby quarry has produced vast quantities of material for railway ballast but otherwise there are few minerals of economic importance on the route.

The line leaves the valley of the River Okement, passes over the headwaters of the west flowing River Thrushel to pursue an undulating course over the upland pastures to Ashbury. A descent at mostly 1 in 78 commences one mile prior to this station and continues almost to Halwill. Further level sections are interspersed with peaks, the maximum gradients being 1 in 78.

An almost continuous descent from Holsworthy to Bude follows, the line running from Devon into Cornwall. It passes over a number of small rivers which flow south into the River Tamar. It crosses the Tamar itself east of Whitstone & Bridgerule and then runs down the valley of the River Strat to its mouth.

The final two miles are across the level marshes south of the holiday resort of Bude, which developed following the arrival of the railway. The Bude Canal, built in 1819-24, was brought into decline upon the arrival of this competitor. Most of the route traverses the Culm Measures, a thick bed of sandstones with siltstones and shales.

All maps are to the scale of 25" to 1 mile and are from the Ordnance Survey second edition of 1905-06, unless otherwise stated.

# HISTORICAL BACKGROUND

The London & South Western Railway's trains began operating westwards to Okehampton from 3rd October 1871. After proposals for a route further east had fallen through, the Devon & Cornwall Railway obtained an Act in 1873 to construct a line from its then incomplete route from Okehampton to Lydford at Meldon Junction, to Holsworthy. Opening to Lydford was on 12th October 1874 and to Holsworthy on 20th January 1879. Both lines were worked by the LSWR from the start and acquired by them in 1874 and 1880 respectively. Proposals to lay lines to Bude from Torrington and Holsworthy both having come to nothing, the LSWR obtained powers to continue from Holsworthy by its Act of 1895 and the line opened on 10th August 1898.

The route south from Halwill to Launceston came into use on 21st July 1886 but the line north to Torrington did not carry traffic until 27th July 1925.

The lines became part of the Southern Railway in 1923 and the Southern Region of British Railways upon nationalisation in 1948. They were transferred to the Western Region on 1st January 1963. Diesel multiple units were introduced to the route on 4th January 1965.

The first closure in the area was the Torrington - Halwill route on 1st March 1965. Meldon Junction to Bude and Halwill Junction to Wadebridge succumbed on 3rd October 1966. Passenger services west of Okehampton ceased on 6th May 1968 while those to the east lasted until 5th June 1972. Stone trains from Meldon Quarry were still running when this book was published in 1994.

# PASSENGER SERVICES

These notes refer to weekday timetables, unless otherwise stated, and to down trains, the up service being similar but often showing one less journey.

The 1881 timetable had six trains per day to Holsworthy, this increasing to eight by 1890. The 11.0am from Waterloo gave an arrival time of 5.11pm and a coach connection to Bude which was reached at 6.50pm.

The initial train service to Bude in 1898 comprised seven journeys, a frequency that was maintained for most of the life of the route. There were slight reductions during the wars and a year or two thereafter and in the final years there were eight journeys per day.

Sunday trains were sparse, there being only one train in the evening for many years, mainly intended for the carriage of the up mails. In most summers from 1938 there were two additional trains during the day. In the early years there were no Sunday trains at all, neither were there after September 1965.

A through coach or coaches from Waterloo ran normally once a day from the Edwardian era through to September 1964. From July 1926 they formed part of the "Atlantic Coast Express", a prestigious train which was often formed of nine portions. However, on summer Saturdays Bude would receive through coaches from up to five trains from Waterloo. These trains and the ACE were among the few not to call at the smaller intermediate stations on the route.

For the summer of 1965 only, a through train to Paddington was operated on Saturdays via Yeovil Pen Mill.

LONDON, EXETER, YEOFORD, OKEHAMPTON, BUDE, WADEBRIDGE, and PADSTOW.

Week Days only.

| Miles | Down. | mrn | E | S | non | mrn | mrn | mrn | mrn | mrn | mrn | aft | aft | aft | aft | aft |
|---|---|---|---|---|---|---|---|---|---|---|---|---|---|---|---|---|
| | | | | | Mondays to Fridays. | | | Mons. to Fris. Restaurant Car, London to Padstow. Atlantic Coast Express. | Saturdays. Restaurant Car, London to Padstow. Atlantic Coast Express. | Sats. Atlantic Coast Express. Restaurant Car, London to Exeter. | Restaurant Car, London to Exeter. | Restaurant Car, London to Exeter (Okehampton on Tues., Weds., and Thurs.) | Saturdays. Restaurant Car, London to Exeter. | Restaurant Car, London to Exeter. Mondays to Fridays. | Restaurant Car, London to Exeter. Saturdays. | Thursdays and Saturdays. |
| | LONDON (Waterloo) 176 dep. | .. | 10V33 | 1220 | F | E | S | 10 35 | 1045 | 11 0 | 11 0 | 12 40 | 2 0 | 3 0 | 3 0 | .. |
| — | Salisbury 170 " | .... | 3 6 | 3 6 | .... | 8 0 | 8 0 | 12 9 | 1229 | 1238 | 12B34 | 2 34 | 3 34 | 4 31 | 4 34 | .... |
| — | Exeter (Central) dep. | .. | 8 46 | 8 46 | .. | 1140 | 1140 | 2 6 | 2 13 | 2 23 | 2C26 | 4 50 | 5 20 | 6 34 | 6 41 | .. |
| 172½ | " (St. David's) arr. | .... | 8 49 | 8 49 | .... | 1143 | 1143 | 2 9 | 2 18 | 2 28 | 2C31 | 4 55 | 5 25 | 6 39 | 6 46 | .... |
| | " (St. David's) dep. | .. | 8 51 | 8 51 | | 1146 | 1144 | 2 11 | 2 20 | 2 29 | 2a33 | 4 57 | 5 27 | 6 41 | 6 47 | |
| 176¾ | Newton St. Cyres | .... | 9 1 | 9 1 | | 1156 | 1153 | | | | .... | .... | .... | .... | .... | |
| 179 | Crediton | .. | 9 7 | 9 7 | | 12 2 | 1159 | | | | .. | .. | .. | 6 53 | 6 59 | |
| 183 | Yeoford arr. | .... | 9 14 | 9 14 | | 1210 | 12 7 | | | | .... | 5 14 | 5 44 | 7 2 | 7 8 | |
| | Yeoford dep. | .. | 9 15 | 9 15 | | 1211 | 12 8 | | | | .. | 5 15 | 5 47 | 7 3 | 7 9 | |
| 187¾ | Bow | .... | 9 24 | 9 24 | | 1221 | 1218 | | | | .... | .... | .... | .... | .... | |
| 191 | North Tawton | .. | 9 31 | 9 31 | | 1228 | 1225 | | | | .. | .. | .. | .. | .. | |
| 193¾ | Sampford Courtenay | .... | 9 37 | 9 37 | | 1235 | 1232 | | | | .... | .... | .... | .... | .... | |
| 197¾ | Okehampton arr. | .. | 9 46 | 9 46 | | 1244 | 1241 | .. | | 3 8 | 3a12 | 5 39 | 6 13 | 7 27 | 7 33 | |
| | Okehampton dep. | .... | 10 0 | 10 0 | | 1 0 | 1 0 | .... | | 3 22 | 3 40 | 5 52 | 6 27 | 7 40 | 7 47 | |
| 202¾ | Maddaford Moor Halt A | .. | 10 13 | 1013 | | 1 13 | 1 13 | .. | | .. | 3 52 | 6 5 | 6 40 | 7 53 | 8 0 | |
| 206½ | Ashbury, for North Lew | .... | 10 21 | 1021 | | 1 21 | 1 21 | .... | | .... | 4 1 | 6 13 | 6 48 | 8 2 | 8 9 | |
| 210¼ | Halwill C (below) arr. | .. | 10 29 | 1029 | | 1 28 | 1 28 | 3 15 | | .. | 4 8 | 6 20 | 6 55 | 8 10 | 8 17 | |
| 230¾ | TORRINGTON arr. | .... | 12 12 | 1212 | | .... | .... | .... | .... | .... | .... | 8E12 | 8 24 | .... | .... | |
| — | Halwill dep. | 8 15 | 10 37 | 1037 | 12 0 | 1 30 | 1 38 | 3 23 | .. | .. | 4 13 | 6 25 | 6 57 | 8 15 | 8 22 | |
| 213½ | Dunsland Cross | 8 21 | 10 45 | 1045 | 12 6 | 1 38 | 1 46 | .... | .... | .... | 4 21 | 6 33 | 7 5 | 8 23 | 8 30 | |
| 218¼ | Holsworthy | 8 30 | 10 56 | 1055 | 1215 | 1 47 | 2 0 | 3 36 | .. | 3 55 | 4 30 | 6 41 | 7 14 | 8 32 | 8 39 | 9 37 |
| 223 | Whitstone and Bridgerule | 8 40 | 11 9 | 11 9 | 1225 | 1 56 | 2 11 | 3 46 | .... | 4 5 | 4 40 | 6 50 | 7 23 | 8 41 | 8 48 | 9 45 |
| 228¾ | Bude arr. | 8 50 | 11 19 | 1119 | 1235 | 2 6 | 2 21 | 3 56 | .. | 4 15 | 4 50 | 7 0 | 7 33 | 8 51 | 8 58 | 9 55 |
| 231¼ | Marhamchurch* arr. | .... | .... | .... | .... | 3 15 | .... | 4 45 | .... | 4 45 | .... | .... | .... | .... | .... | .... |
| 230 | Stratton* " | 10 8 | 11 55 | 1155 | .. | 3 0 | .. | 4 30 | .. | 4 30 | 6 30 | .. | .. | 9 6 | 9 6 | .. |
| 233¼ | Widemouth Bay* " | 9 45 | 11 42 | 1142 | 1 45 | 3 30 | .... | 4 32 | .... | 4 32 | 5 17 | 7 47 | .... | .... | .... | .... |
| — | Halwill dep. | Stop | 10 30 | 1030 | .. | 1 34 | 1 34 | 3 18 | .. | | 4 10 | 6 21 | 7 1 | 8 11 | 8 18 | .. |
| 215¼ | Ashwater | | 10 40 | 1040 | .... | 1 43 | 1 43 | .... | .... | | 4 19 | 6 31 | 7 11 | 8 21 | 8 28 | .... |
| 219 | Tower Hill | mrn | 10 47 | 1047 | .. | 1 50 | 1 50 | .. | .. | | 4 29 | 6 38 | 7 17 | 8 28 | 8 35 | .. |
| 224 | Launceston 62 | 7 45 | 10 56 | 1056 | .... | 1 59 | 1 59 | 3 39 | 3 35 | | 4 42 | 6 48 | 7 26 | 8 37 | 8 44 | .... |
| 228¼ | Egloskerry | 7 53 | 11 7 | 11 7 | .. | 2 9 | 2 9 | .. | .. | | 4 50 | 7 2 | 7 35 | | 8 54 | .. |
| 231¾ | Tresmeer | 8 2 | 11 15 | 1115 | .... | 2 17 | 2 17 | .... | .... | | 4 58 | 7 13 | 7 43 | | 9 2 | .... |
| 236¾ | Otterham B | 8 12 | 11 25 | 1126 | .. | 2 27 | 2 27 | 4 5 | 4 3 | | 5 8 | 7 23 | 7 53 | | 9 12 | .. |
| 241¼ | Camelford F | 8 21 | 11 33 | 1137 | .... | 2 35 | 2 35 | 4 14 | 4 13 | | 5 17 | 7 31 | 8 1 | | 9 20 | .... |
| 246¼ | Tintagel* arr. | .. | .. | .. | .. | .. | .. | .. | .. | | .. | .. | .. | | .. | .. |
| 245¾ | Boscastle* " | .... | .... | .... | .... | .... | .... | .... | .... | | .... | .... | .... | | .... | .... |
| 243½ | Delabole | 8 27 | 11 39 | 1143 | .. | 2 41 | 2 41 | 4 21 | 4 22 | | 5 23 | 7 37 | 8 8 | | 9 26 | .. |
| 247¾ | Port Isaac Road | 8 35 | 11 46 | 1150 | .... | 2 49 | 2 49 | 4 29 | 4 30 | | 5 31 | 7 45 | 8 16 | | | .... |
| 250¼ | St. Kew Highway | 8 40 | 11 51 | 1155 | .. | 2 54 | 2 54 | .. | .. | | 5 36 | 7 50 | 8 21 | | | .. |
| 254½ | Wadebridge 179 arr. | 8 48 | 11 58 | 12 2 | .... | 3 2 | 3 2 | 4 40 | 4 44 | | 5 44 | 7 58 | 8 29 | | | .... |
| 270 | Newquay* arr. | 11E15 | 1 40 | 1 40 | .. | .. | .. | 6 15 | 6 15 | | 7 35 | .. | .. | | | .. |
| — | Wadebridge dep. | 8 50 | 12 0 | 12 4 | .... | 3 21 | 3 21 | 4 43 | 4 46 | | 5 59 | 7 59 | 8 29 | .... | | .... |
| 260 | Padstow arr. | 9 1 | 12 11 | 1215 | .. | 3 31 | 3 31 | 4 53 | 4 57 | | 6 9 | 8 9 | 8 40 | .. | | .. |
| 266 | Bedruthan* arr. | .... | .... | .... | .... | .... | .... | 7 10 | 7 10 | | .... | .... | .... | .... | | .... |
| 262 | Trevone Bay* " | 9H20 | 2 20 | 2 20 | .. | .. | .. | 5 20 | 5 20 | | .. | 9E40 | 9 40 | .. | | .. |

A For Thorndon Cross.
a 4 mins. *earlier* on Sats.
B For Wilsey Down and Davidstow (2½ miles) and Crackington Haven (5 mls.)
B 4 mins. later on Sats.
C For Beaworthy.
C 3 mins. *earlier* on Sats.

E or E Mons. to Fris.
F For Boscastle and Tintagel.
F Friday midnight to 7th Sept. only. Dep. 10 33 aft. on Friday nights commencing 14th Sept. via Eastleigh.

H Arr. 9 55 mrn. on Sats.
S or S Saturdays.
V Via Eastleigh, Mons., Tues., and Thurs. nights. On Weds. dep. 12 5 midnight direct.
* By Southern National Motor Omnibus. Times subject to alteration.

August 1934

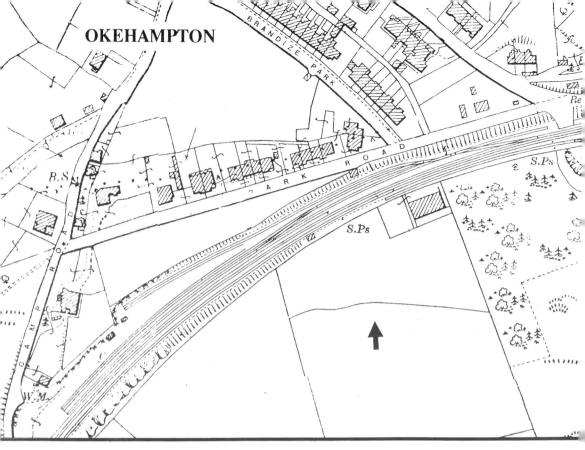

# OKEHAMPTON

1. The station was the terminus of the route from Exeter from 3rd October 1871 to 12th October 1874 when operations were extended to Lydford. This staff photograph shows the down side before it received a canopy. The sign on the right reads *REFRESHMENTS ROOM*. (Lens of Sutton)

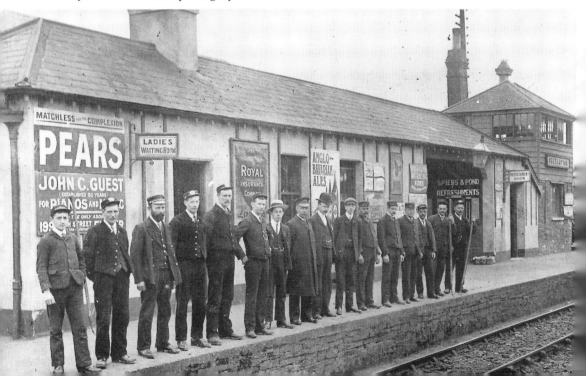

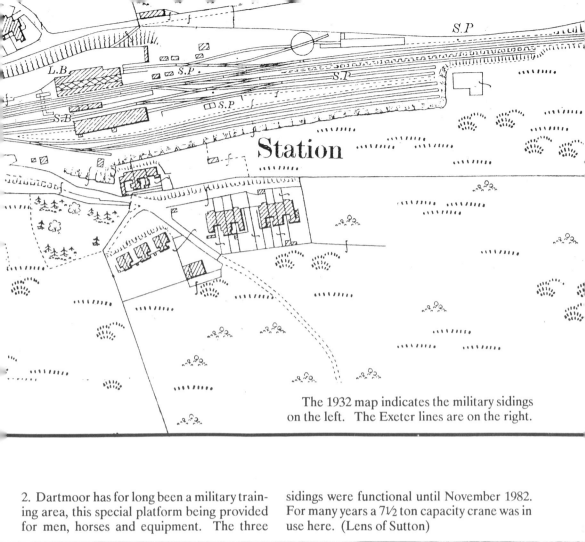

The 1932 map indicates the military sidings on the left. The Exeter lines are on the right.

2. Dartmoor has for long been a military training area, this special platform being provided for men, horses and equipment. The three sidings were functional until November 1982. For many years a 7½ ton capacity crane was in use here. (Lens of Sutton)

3. The station was built on a shelf between the steep northern slope of Dartmoor and the town, which once had a productive tanyard and a boot and shoe manufacturer. The grammar school also generated railway traffic.
(Lens of Sutton)

5. The water column featured in the previous picture is seen again to the right of class 0415 4-4-2T no. 125 on 14th July 1924. A few of these locomotives came to the area in 1916 following electrification of some suburban lines. The coach is devoid of wheels, having been grounded as staff accommodation.
(H.C.Casserley)

4. The locomotive shed is seen in August 1928 with a wagon over the pit while it is loaded with ash. The first shed was built with timber in about 1895, and was burnt down in 1920 to be replaced by this structure constructed from concrete blocks. No. E029 was of class 0395 and was renumbered 3029 in 1931 and 30564 in 1948. (H.C.Casserley)

6. An eastward panorama from the signal post included in the last picture shows the layout in 1938. The two sidings nearest the main line were extended in 1939 and the 50ft. turntable was replaced by a 70ft one nearer the up platform in November 1947. (W.A.Camwell)

7. A westward view includes the canopy that was added to the building featured in picture no.1 and also the roof of the massive goods shed. (The canopy supports are pre-cast concrete components). This and the next two pictures were taken on 28th August 1945. (H.C.Casserley)

9. Waiting in the down bay is class L11 no. 156 which had been built in 1903 with unusual cross firebox watertubes. The size of the goods shed reflected the relative importance of this traffic here. (H.C.Casserley)

8. An up stone train includes coach no. 6551 for the benefit of quarry workers. The locomotive is class T9 4-4-0 no. 724, its large tender being a reminder of the fact the SR was alone amongst the big companies in having no water troughs for its expresses. (H.C.Casserley)

SOUTHERN RAILWAY.
Issued subject to the Bye-laws, Regulations & Conditions in the Company's Bills and Notices.

7985   Okehampton   to   7985
Okehampton                    Okehampton
Maddaford Moor Halt          Maddaford Moor Halt
**MADDAFORD MOOR HALT**
THIRD CLASS          THIRD CLASS
Fare 1/1½            Fare 1/1½
NOT TRANSFERABLE

10. The addition of roofs to the footbridge and platforms must have been welcome in this area of high rainfall on the lee of Dartmoor. This illustration reveals the platform numbering employed. (Lens of Sutton)

12. On 4th June 1959 the 9.56am departure for Bude and Padstow was composed of five coaches and an ex-LMS six-wheeled van. With a train of this length class T9 no. 30717 was ahead of the starting signal, which is behind the van. (J.H.Aston)

11. The 1.18pm departure for Bude on 3rd June 1959 was worked by class T9 no. 30726 and was composed of Maunsell designed coaches from the inter-war years. The connecting train was the 11.47am from Exeter Central, which arrived at 12.53 and proceeded to Plymouth. (S.C.Nash)

13. Included in this view across the Okement Valley is a bowler-hatted inspector waiting to leave on the 9.56am on 15th July 1960. This is the same departure, location and locomotive class as in the previous picture. (R.C.Riley)

14. The signal box was on the up platform and was in use from 12th May 1935 until 10th July 1972. Its predecessor was on the down and is illustrated in picture no.1. After closure, the building was used for a period as an office by a coach operator. (Wessex collection)

British Railways Board (W)
OKEHAMPTON
PLATFORM TICKET 3d.
Available one hour on day of issue only
Not valid in trains. Not transferable
To be given up when leaving platform
For conditions see over

1 2 3 4 5 6

15. Although giving the impression of a single storey building when seen from the up platform, the rear view presented a different story. It emphasises the fact that the station was constructed on a hillside shelf and that the siting of the first box was the easy option, albeit on the inside of the curve with less satisfactory visibility. (Wessex collection)

16. The substantial goods shed had no less than three pairs of doors for road vehicles but those over the siding are missing. A Motorail car-carrying service operated from Surbiton in the summers of 1960-64 but this used the docks shown in picture no.2. Goods services ceased in 1979. (Wessex collection)

17. The up side buildings were rebuilt in 1928 but still contained the traditional letter box in the wall. Regular passenger services ceased on 5th June 1972 when the Exeter trains were withdrawn. In the mid-1980s some DMUs were run for ramblers and pre-Christmas shoppers. Earlier, there had been some others run in connection with coach tours of closed stations. (Wessex collection)

18. The revised turntable position is seen from the end of the up platform on 3rd October 1964, the locomotive shed being in the distance, unaltered. The locomotives are BR class 4 2-6-4Ts which were introduced to the area in May 1962. Note that shelters were provided on the coal stage and over the turntable handwheel. (C.L.Caddy)

19. After closure to passengers a loop was retained, the down platform being in the centre of it. The line to Meldon Quarry had been singled on 22nd March 1970 and that to Crediton on 17th October 1971. By 1994 all stone trains passed through the up platform but several sidings were still in place, two lines forming a loop round the down platform. (Lens of Sutton)

# WEST OF OKEHAMPTON

20. A Bude to Tynemouth Territorial Army troop special was recorded on the descent to Okehampton on 31st July 1959, with class N no. 31843 as train engine and class T9 no. 30338 as pilot. Two N class coupled together were banned over Meldon Viaduct. (S.C.Nash)

# MELDON QUARRY

A small quarry was worked for local railway requirements in 1874 but it was not until 1897 that it was developed to provide most of the LSWR's ballast. Within a few years it was producing over 100,000 tons per annum. The 1905 map shows several short and movable 2ft. gauge lines and four staff cottages. These were increased to twelve by 1907. By 1953, 340,000 tons of ballast were produced in the year for use on the Southern Region. Uncertainties following transfer to the Western Region proved unfounded as that area also took the quarry's products. In 1993 Network South-East changed to Scottish ballast conveyed by sea to Grain (see our *Branch Line to Allhallows*) and the quarry was sold to ECC Quarries Ltd on 4th March 1994, along with the line through Okehampton as far as the site of Coleford Junction.

S.P

Ancient Trackway
(Site of)

*Meldon Quarry*

S.P

S.B

S.P

S.P

*Meldon Quarry Cottages*

*Meldon Viaduct*

21. For many years horses provided motive power within the quarry and shunting engines were sent from Exeter as required. In 1927 Manning Wardle 0-4-0ST no. 313 was allocated to the quarry, becoming no. 225S. It had been built for the SER in 1881 and worked at Folkestone Harbour most of its life before transfer to Meldon where it was active until 1938. It was photographed in August 1928. (H.C.Casserley)

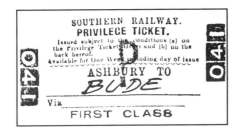

22. After trials with a class B4 0-4-0T and an O2 0-4-4T, ex-SECR class T 0-6-0T no. 1607 was sent to the quarry in September 1938, renumbered 500S and used there until 1948. Class 02 no. 199 was recorded in August 1945 on temporary assignment, alongside the loading bins. (H.C.Casserley)

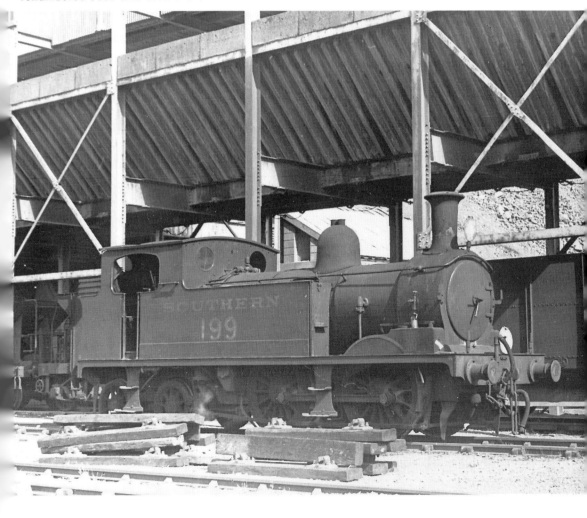

23. A further eight acres of Dartmoor were acquired in 1902 and the site eventually covered 200 acres. This 1948 eastward view includes the crushers and screens. The narrow gauge railway was abandoned in the following year and the quarry was soon producing over 300,000 tons per annum. (J.H.Aston)

24. Class 02 no. 232 was in the decaying shed on 6th June 1948. The hopper wagons seen are of 20-ton capacity but 40-ton bogie vehicles were also in use. Output was mostly track ballast but large tonnages of packing chippings were produced along with finer materials for the Exmouth Junction Concrete Works. (J.H.Aston)

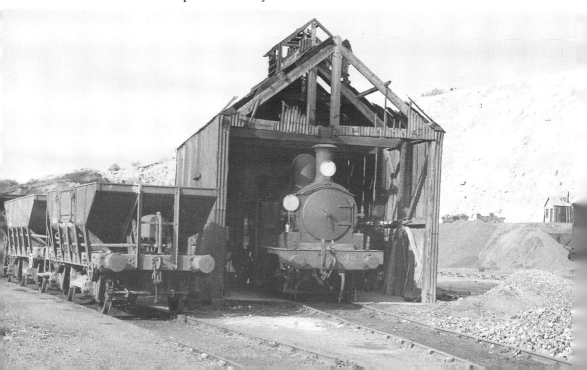

25. A glimpse from an up train on 20th August 1954 includes the staff platform, the water tank, an excavator and class G6 0-6-0T no. DS3152, ex-LSWR no. 272. It worked at the quarry from November 1949 until July 1960. Another G6 (DS682 ex-BR no. 30238) ran here from November 1960 to December 1962, when USA 0-6-0T no. DS234 took over. Class 08 diesel shunters were introduced in October 1966. (H.C.Casserley)

26. A down freight for the North Cornwall line was headed by class N no. 31847 on 3rd June 1959 and is passing under the bridge which was built at the east end of the site for the conveyance of overburden and topsoil to a dump area. The reservoir on the right supplied water for ballast washing and also for Okehampton station and shed. (S.C.Nash)

27. No. DS3152 is coupled to class T9 no. 30726 on 4th June 1959. They are propelling loaded bogie wagons out on to the down main line, together with the coach provided for staff and families resident in the quarry cottages. The assistance was needed on account of the 1 in 77 gradient. (J.H.Aston)

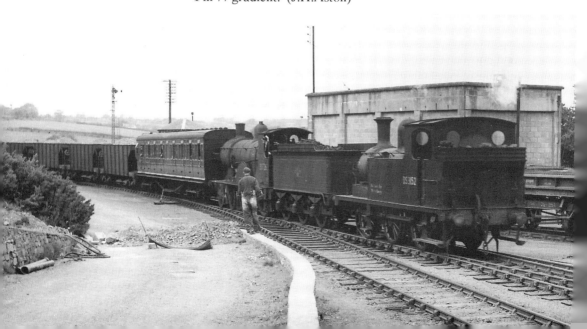

28. A few minutes later no. 30726 hauls its train over the crossover onto the up line, having shed the shunter. The signal box windows had been protected from flying debris when the quarry face was nearer to it. Blasting was not allowed when trains were passing. (J.H.Aston)

29. No. 08584 pulls DACE wagons after loading in August 1989. Stone carrying wagons have for long been named after marine creatures. The building on the left is the engine shed. (J.A.M.Vaughan)

# MELDON VIADUCT

CATCH POINTS

30. An elegant locomotive on an elegant structure was captured on film on 14th July 1924. Carrying the Plymouth headcode, class T9 no. E117 still has sandboxes on its leading splasher as fitted to the first engines of this class and later removed. (H.C.Casserley)

31. Steam largely obscures the viaduct which class T9 no. 30726 has just crossed on 4th June 1959, but the quarry is evident in the background. The line on the viaduct is at 1 in 77 but this increases to 1 in 58, hence the need for catch points. (J.H.Aston)

32. Details of the slender 150ft high structure were recorded in August 1960, along with the staff footbridge. The spans can be seen to be at an angle to one another as the entire structure was built on a 30-chain curve. (E.W.Fry)

33. The up line over the viaduct was taken out of use on 24th April 1966, the down being retained for traffic until 6th May 1968. Part of this line on the viaduct was kept as a headshunt for quarry trains but it now carries no track. The more recent expansion of the quarry plant is apparent. (C.Hall)

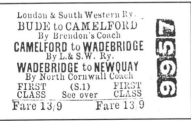

London & South Western Ry.
BUDE to CAMELFORD
By Brendon's Coach
CAMELFORD to WADEBRIDGE
By L.& S.W. Ry.
WADEBRIDGE to NEWQUAY
By North Cornwall Coach
FIRST (S.1) FIRST
CLASS See over CLASS
Fare 13/9        Fare 13/9

3rd-SINGLE        SINGLE-3rd
BUDE to
BUDE                                BUDE
Halwill                          Halwill
HALWILL
(W) 2/10 FARE 2/10 (W)
ForConditions see over ForConditions see over

34. With the mass of Dartmoor in the background, class T9 no. 30313 leaves the Plymouth line (right) and heads for Padstow with the 5.51pm from Okehampton on 12th May 1961, the last year that this class could be seen regularly in the area. The summit of the route at over 900ft. above sea level was on this 15-chain curve. (S.C.Nash)

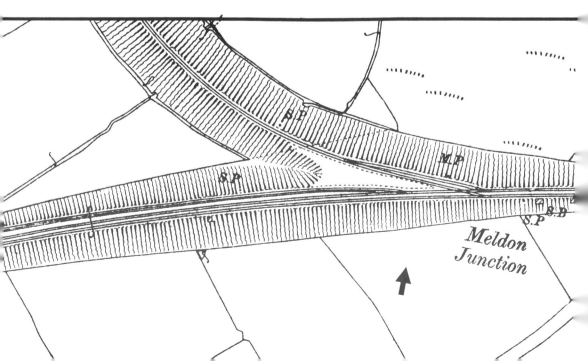

35. The double track to Plymouth is straight on as a DMU takes to the single line to Halwill on 13th June 1966. The single line tablet is devoid of the usual pouch and hoop. (D.Cullum coll.)

The siding on the left and the loop on the right were used for transfer goods traffic between the Plymouth and the Bude/Padstow lines until about 1930 when the improved Exmouth Junction marshalling yard took over the work. The loop was reinstated in 1943 for wartime traffic and remained usable until 1965.

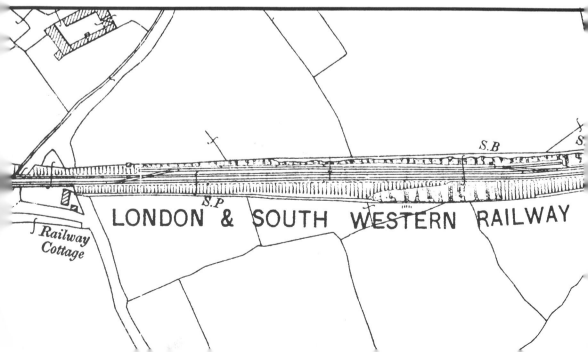

# MADDAFORD MOOR HALT

36. The halt was opened on 27th July 1926 and was equipped with a durable concrete name-board cast at the SR's Exmouth Junction Concrete Works. Few lived in the vicinity but there was a terrace of railwaymen's cottages nearby. (Lens of Sutton)

38. A passing loop was situated here from 1899 until 4th August 1921, the signal box being located north of the later platform site. A DMU stands at the platform, shortly before line closure. The following pictures were taken near the halt. (Wessex collection)

37. Less durable was the waiting shed, carefully named so that passengers were aware of its intended function. The guard would attend to platform lighting as necessary. (Wessex collection)

39. The moor made a good location to record the royal train running up from Launceston on 9th May 1956, with the special exclusive headcode. The N class locomotives (nos. 31830 and 31845) presumably had special permission to cross Meldon Viaduct together. There are many six-wheeled bogies to be seen. (S.C.Nash)

40. The Padstow portion of the much divided ACE was photographed on 12th May 1961, headed by no. 34110 *66 Squadron*. These Bulleid Pacifics seldom ran to Bude, as they were too long for the turntable there. The Bude coaches of the ACE were detached at Halwill. (S.C.Nash)

41. The N class was equally suited to royal trains as to freight trains. First seen in the district in 1924, they were so successful that they worked to the end of steam in the area in 1964. No. 31874 plods uphill on 8th May 1961. (S.C.Nash)

42. Venn Gates box and cottage were situated less than one mile from the halt. The only other public crossing on the branch was at Halwill. (Wessex collection)

# ASHBURY

43. A poor quality postcard at least features the fine tapered wooden signal post not seen in other views. The headcode is a diamond by the chimney and a disc in the centre of the buffer beam. In 1905 this indicated Exeter - Padstow. (Lens of Sutton)

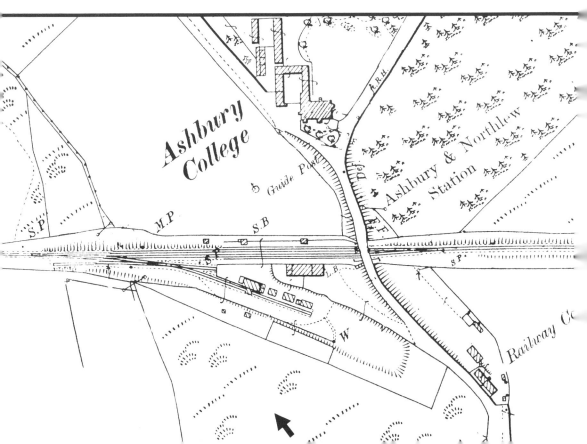

44. The station master, wife, child and porter pose at their well kept station. The rockery was whitewashed but the platform edge was not. Note the alternative to the chimney pots seen in later photographs. (Lens of Sutton)

45. The rockery and shrubs have gone, no doubt as a result of SR standardisation but their poster boards are in profusion. There are ten visible but fewer than seven tickets were issued on an average day in 1936.
(Lens of Sutton)

| Ashbury | 1928 | 1936 |
|---|---|---|
| No. of passenger tickets issued | 6141 | 2363 |
| No. of season tickets issued | 30 | 26 |
| No. of tickets collected | 6424 | 3774 |
| No. of telegrams | 370 | 112 |
| Parcels forwarded | 1354 | 775 |
| Parcels received | 972 | 1135 |
| Horses forwarded | 4 | 32 |
| Milk forwarded - cans 1928/gallons 1936 | 51 | - |
| Milk received - cans 1928/gallons 1936 | - | - |
| General goods forwarded (tons) | 263 | 845 |
| General goods received (tons) | 1632 | 1603 |
| Coal, Coke etc. received (tons) | 373 | 337 |
| Other minerals forwarded (tons) | - | - |
| Other minerals received (tons) | 2381 | 1077 |
| Trucks livestock forwarded | 62 | 46 |
| Trucks livestock received | 18 | 5 |
| Lavatory pennies | - | 11 |

SOUTHERN RAILWAY.
This Ticket is issued subject to the By-laws Regulations & Conditions stated in the Company's Time Tables Bills & Notices
ASHBURY to
HALWILL
Via
1st Class       Fare 9.

2nd - SINGLE       SINGLE 2nd
Ashbury  to
Ashbury
Halwill
HALWILL
(S) 8d       FARE       8d (S)
For condit'ns see over   For condit'ns see over

5324        5

46. The station came to life intermittently, such as when the 5.10pm Okehampton to Bude called on 23rd July 1964. Power was provided by class 4 2-6-4T no. 80059, a very successful design. (J.H.Aston)

47. No intermediate stations on the route were provided with footbridges but here there was a choice of the road bridge or the crossing seen in the previous picture. The oil lamp is in place in the lantern, an ornate but ineffective combination. (Wessex collection)

48. Devoid of its lamp, this lantern has one glass showing the station name. The lamp will be in the lamp hut which will also contain a drum of oil, a bench, a can with spout and a pair of scissors for wick trimming. (Wessex collection)

49. This panorama includes the warehouse, the goods shed, the porch of the dwelling area, the letter box and the up platform shelter - almost everything that was required at a minor country station, except passengers. (Wessex collection)

50. This is the second store, not visible in the previous view. Such buildings were erected at most rural stations by distributors of artificial fertilisers and animal feedstuffs, and also seed merchants. (Wessex collection)

51. At the end of the goods shed was the paved area and fence posts of the former cattle pen. Railwaymen were not sorry to see the end of this traffic in the early 1960s. The cleaning of wagons and pens, along with the problems of sick or dead animals were never welcome. (Wessex collection)

52.  A DMU stands with smoke coming from its engine.  The far end of the loop had been extended in October 1936 to cope with the longer trains in the holiday seasons.  This is the original signal box and it had ten levers, one of which was spare.  (Wessex Collection)

53.  As at a number of small stations, the signal box was extended to accommodate booking facilities, thus making it easier for one man to operate the station. The outside bell was of value when he was attending to goods traffic or the labour intensive lamps.
(Wessex collection)

54.  Goods service at the shed in the background ceased on 7th September 1964 and after total closure in 1966 the premises were converted into a desirable residence. (C.Hall)

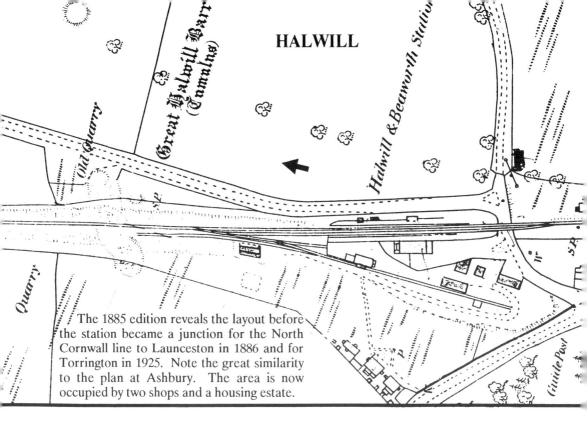

# HALWILL

The 1885 edition reveals the layout before the station became a junction for the North Cornwall line to Launceston in 1886 and for Torrington in 1925. Note the great similarity to the plan at Ashbury. The area is now occupied by two shops and a housing estate.

55. The name on the map was used until March 1887 when "Halwill Junction" was adopted. The old name is still shown as a Padstow to Exeter train waits for the signal to clear. The lower quadrant signals lasted until 1934. (Lens of Sutton)

56. Features of note in this posed postcard view are the junction starting signals and the array of point rods cranking under the platform ramp. The Torrington line was laid later on their site. (Lens of Sutton)

57. A down goods train parted on its descent to the station on 3rd February 1905. The driver arrived with the front portion unaware that the guard was trying to retard the rear section. This crashed into the former on the level crossing causing fatalities amongst some pigs, injuries to two railwaymen and damage to 25 wagons. (Lens of Sutton)

58.  Seen near the goods shed on 16th June 1926 is class 0460 4-4-0 no. 0468. Designed by Adams and built in 1884, it lasted until 1929 having been used initially on express services. The lattice signal post was an LSWR feature. (H.C.Casserley)

59.  "Halwill for Beaworthy" is the name shown in this view from the early SR era. It is remarkable that no platform shelters or footbridge were erected at this junction station. The population of Halwill dropped from 418 in 1891 to 382 in 1951. Depopulation in earlier years had not encouraged railway development. (Lens of Sutton)

60. The 10.0am from Okehampton leaves the single line section on 12th May 1939, hauled by N class 2-6-0 no 1845. The Padstow portion would leave at 10.30 and the Bude coaches at 10.37. The accident picture (no. 57) was taken from almost the same position. (J.R.W.Kirkby)

61. A few minutes later, the Bude portion leaves behind class L11 4-4-0 no. 175. On the right is the LSWR's slaughterhouse, one of several built on the system to generate traffic. They were taken over by the Ministry of Food during World War I and subsequently sold to local companies. (J.R.W.Kirkby)

62. In the foreground is the Torrington line platform which was added in 1925. Class E1/R 0-6-2T no. 32696 waits to depart at 10.40am on 16th June 1950. Meat vans stand at the slaughterhouse which in 1932 had dealt with 48,000 animals. The 5.0pm "perishables" departure left wagons at Templecombe for the Midlands, the rest arriving at Nine Elms in the small hours. The meat was in the London Markets by 4.0am. In drought conditions water was taken from here to Holsworthy in the old SER locomotive tender seen on the right. (J.J.Smith)

| Halwill | 1928 | 1936 |
|---|---|---|
| No. of passenger tickets issued | 11016 | 5753 |
| No. of season tickets issued | 36 | 37 |
| No. of tickets collected | 11483 | 5706 |
| No. of telegrams | 17040 | 19041 |
| Parcels forwarded | 2426 | 1750 |
| Parcels received | 2123 | 1774 |
| Horses forwarded | 24 | 14 |
| Milk forwarded  - cans 1928/gallons 1936 | 2073 | 3555 |
| Milk received - cans 1928/gallons 1936 | - | - |
| General goods forwarded (tons) | 1586 | 1660 |
| General goods received (tons) | 1473 | 2016 |
| Coal, Coke etc. received (tons) | 496 | 395 |
| Other minerals forwarded (tons) | 36 | 12 |
| Other minerals received (tons) | 1492 | 1896 |
| Trucks livestock forwarded | 364 | 359 |
| Trucks livestock received | 748 | 489 |
| Lavatory pennies | 1726 | 937 |

7547
SOUTHERN RAILWAY.
CHEAP DAY
Available as advertised
Okehampton to
HALWILL
Third Class
FOR CONDITIONS SEE BACK
SOUTHERN RAILWAY.
CHEAP DAY
Available as advertised
Halwill
Okehampton
Halwill to
OKEHAMPTON
Third Class
7547

63. The North Devon & Cornwall Junction Light Railway was the grand title for the little line to Torrington, which became part of the SR and had an independent single track (right) parallel to the Bude line for 300 yards. There was a connection between them, just beyond the locomotives in this 1959 view. (Unknown)

64. The lofty signal box housed four single line instruments for the radiating lines, the tablets being lowered to platform staff by ropes over pulleys. Class 4 2-6-4T heads the 5.10pm Okehampton to Bude on 23rd July 1964. (J.H.Aston)

65. Recorded on 17th July 1964 is the 5.51pm from Okehampton to Padstow (centre) arriving at 6.21. On the left is class 2 no. 41290 with the 6.30 to Torrington (one of only two trains per day), while class 4 no. 80037 waits in the bay with the 6.25 to Bude. The joining of

trains involved the engine of the Bude arrival running round its train, drawing it back onto the branch, waiting for the arrival of the Padstow portion and then propelling the coaches on to it. (R.Palmer)

SOUTHERN RAILWAY.
This Ticket is issued subject to the By-laws Regulations & Conditions stated in the Company's Time Tables Bills & Notices
Available on day of issue only
HALWILL to
BARNSTAPLE
Via Torrington

Halwill
Barnstaple
3rd CLASS
Fare 4/4

Halwill
Barnstaple
3rd CLASS
Fare 4/4

0027

0027

66. The name was officially plain "Halwill" from 1st January 1923, although the cast concrete nameboard was rather more helpful. A spacious house was provided for the station master at this important location. The district is now known as "Halwill Junction". (Lens of Sutton)

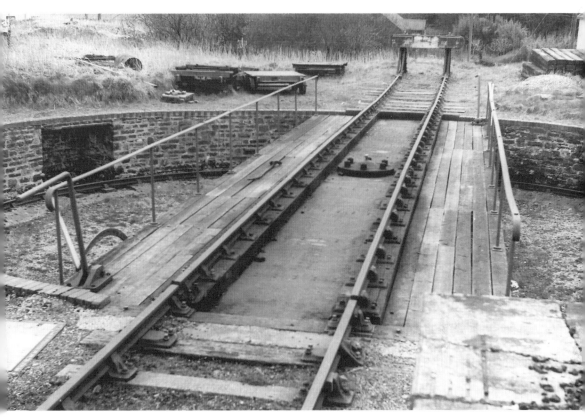

68. The 50ft turntable was little used in its final years owing to its small size and the introduction of tank engines. Its location can be seen in picture 62 - above the container wagon. (Wessex collection)

67. A hut was provided for the gatekeeper who worked the gates by hand. Nine sidings for the War Department were laid beyond the crossing on the left. They were brought into use on 26th March 1943 and most were in place until 1963, their site now being a sports field. (Wessex collection)

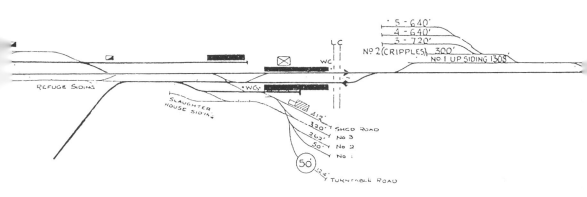

69. In addition to the goods shed, Bibbys had a concrete built store (right) for cattle feeds and Silcocks had an iron clad structure for fertilisers. Goods outward included hides from the slaughterhouse destined for tanneries, rabbits and eggs - as many as 100,000 of the latter in 1932. (Wessex collection)

2nd · SINGLE     SINGLE · 2nd
Halwill to

Halwill               Halwill
Holsworthy          Holsworthy

**HOLSWORHTY**

(W   1/4    Fare    1/4   (W)
For conditions see over   For conditions see over

3964                   3964

70. The fire buckets were hung on the outside of the gentlemen's toilets, as the tap for filling them was therein. The bay platform would accommodate only three coaches. The parallel siding to the end loading dock was removed in 1930 and the goods yard closed on 5th September 1964. (Wessex collection)

71. The Torrington line closed in 1965 and the track was lifted at its southern end in May 1966. This subsequent view shows the trackwork that allowed a Padstow train to leave the bay at the same time as a Bude service from the down platform, although this was not common practice. (Lens of Sutton)

# DUNSLAND CROSS

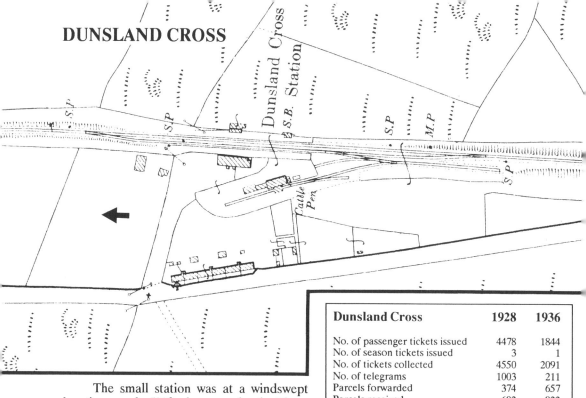

Dunsland Cross

Dunsland Cross S.B. Station

Cattle Pen

The small station was at a windswept location nearly 500ft above sea level. There were few inhabitants in the area, apart from those in the railway terrace marked.

72. The line from Halwill is descending at 1 in 78 on to the short level section through the station. The solitary siding is also level. The SR publicity department was over zealous at this quiet location, as at Ashbury.
(H.C.Casserley coll.)

| Dunsland Cross | 1928 | 1936 |
|---|---|---|
| No. of passenger tickets issued | 4478 | 1844 |
| No. of season tickets issued | 3 | 1 |
| No. of tickets collected | 4550 | 2091 |
| No. of telegrams | 1003 | 211 |
| Parcels forwarded | 374 | 657 |
| Parcels received | 693 | 932 |
| Horses forwarded | 7 | 19 |
| Milk forwarded - cans 1928/gallons 1936 | - | - |
| Milk received - cans 1928/gallons 1936 | - | - |
| General goods forwarded (tons) | 261 | 106 |
| General goods received (tons) | 662 | 294 |
| Coal, Coke etc. received (tons | 449 | 950 |
| Other minerals forwarded (tons) | - | - |
| Other minerals received (tons) | 3271 | 861 |
| Trucks livestock forwarded | 40 | 15 |
| Trucks livestock received | 3 | 14 |
| Lavatory pennies | - | 18 |

73. The up platform shelter was well built to withstand the gales frequently encountered at this upland location. (Wessex collection)

74. As the shadows lengthen, class 4 no. 80037 waits with the 5.35pm Bude to Halwill on 17th July 1964. The single line instruments were moved from the 10-lever signal box to the booking office in the 1920s. The passing of trains was seldom scheduled here. (R.Palmer)

75. The "college", a boys school, brought occasional peaks in traffic. The up line was taken out of use on 2nd January 1966, as a prelude to closure. Unlike Ashbury, the residential part of the building was nearest the camera. (Wessex collection)

76. Bibby's store for rail-borne cattle feedstuffs is to the right of the goods shed. Goods inward included roadstone and also sea sand from Bude Wharf which was used for land improvement owing to its high lime content. Freight facilities were withdrawn on 5th September 1964. The railway cottages are in the background. (Wessex collection)

# HOLSWORTHY

77. The descent to the station was at 1 in 78 over Holsworthy Viaduct although this postcard gives the impression of a rising gradient. The long dark building on the left is the engine shed, for which closure dates of 1st January 1911 and 10th October 1915 are on record. Maybe it reopened without note between these dates. Cole's Mill is in the foreground and lower right on the map. (Lens of Sutton)

78. The station was a terminus from 1879 until 1898 and only the right platform existed in that period. The Bude line is seen to drop away on a curve. Prior to its opening there was a straight terminal line with a turntable siding from it. The 42ft turntable was relocated in front of the engine shed in 1898. (D.Cullum coll.)

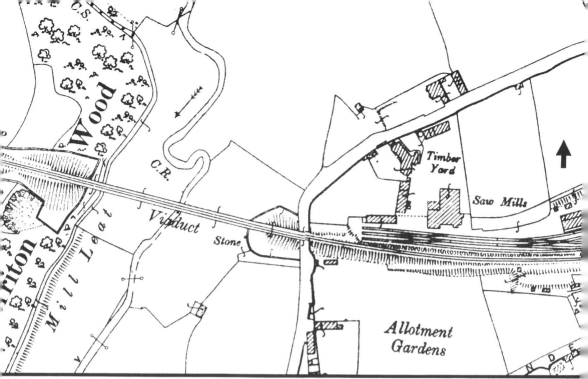

Included on the 1905 map are both viaducts, the engine shed with turntable and the all important railway abattoir, below the north point arrow. The cattle market was established in 1906.

79. The exterior was photographed on 1st February 1900 on the occasion of the official welcome to Mr H.F. Luttrell M.P. The population was only about 1500 for most of the life of the line. (Lens of Sutton)

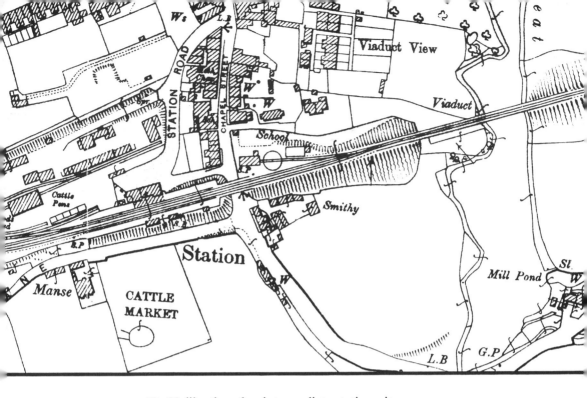

80. Unlike the other intermediate stations, it appears that Holsworthy was provided with this generous awning from the outset. Here we witness the passing of the 5.10pm from Okehampton (right) and the 5.35 from Bude on 23rd July 1964. (J.H.Aston)

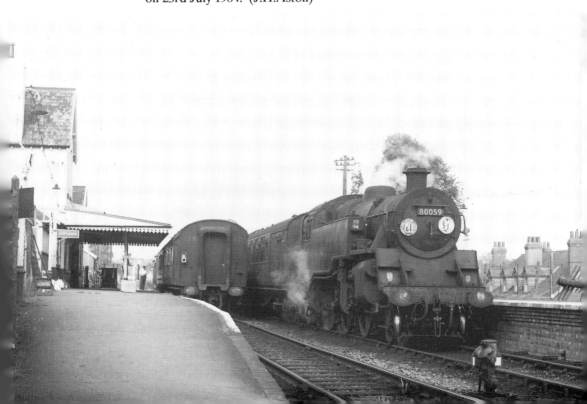

| Holsworthy | 1928 | 1936 |
|---|---|---|
| No. of passenger tickets issued | 17542 | 7990 |
| No. of season tickets issued | 134 | 170 |
| No. of tickets collected | 32922 | 16325 |
| No. of telegrams | 2548 | 2446 |
| Parcels forwarded | 6674 | 4108 |
| Parcels received | 11957 | 13486 |
| Horses forwarded | 114 | 98 |
| Milk forwarded - cans 1928/gallons 1936 | - | - |
| Milk received - cans 1928/gallons 1936 | - | - |
| General goods forwarded (tons) | 2765 | 2203 |
| General goods received (tons) | 11462 | 13327 |
| Coal, Coke etc. received (tons) | 3912 | 3474 |
| Other minerals forwarded (tons) | 43 | 68 |
| Other minerals received (tons) | 9686 | 8772 |
| Trucks livestock forwarded | 1074 | 774 |
| Trucks livestock received | 194 | 57 |
| Lavatory pennies | 1764 | 1720 |

81. The cattle wagon is a reminder that live animals take up more train space than carcasses and so fast overnight carriage of meat to city centres was preferable. A guard recounted how, on one dark wet night here and with raincoat collar upturned, he stooped to read a cattle wagon label and received down his neck a large visiting card from a nervous cow. (C.L.Caddy)

82. The first signal box had 10 levers but the extension of 1898 justified a new box with 20 levers. The brick faced platform was of the same date and contrasted with its stone faced partner on the up side. (E.W.Fry)

83. The eight arch structure over a small stream was built from local stone in 1878 and was photographed shortly before closure. The parapets were removed subsequently. Water was pumped from the stream to supply the station but the source was not reliable in the summer. The exposed position of the signal box is evident. (Wessex collection)

84. The station master's residence occupied most of the two-storey part of the premises, the tall chimney and pot being on his wife's washhouse. The rear-engined Hillman Imp and handcart at the parcel office door add a period flavour. (Wessex collection)

85. The LSWR lattice post had an SR upper quadrant arm fitted to it, probably in the mid-1930s. Bridge 33 was over Chapel Street. Many animals walked under this bridge to be loaded onto trains, dead or alive. (Wessex collection)

86. The slaughterhouse is obscured in this view of the goods shed but it did provide traffic other than meat, such as sheepskins to Buckfastleigh, fat to a candlemaker in Exeter and gut to Birmingham. Wool was handled in the early years and in the 1940s and 50s sugar beet was loaded for Ely and Kidderminster. The shed was fitted with a 2-ton crane. (Wessex collection)

87. Freight traffic ceased on 5th September 1964, Halwill and Holsworthy having been the only stations for livestock on the route since 1st January 1963. The fuel filler is a reminder that petrol depots were established south of the line in the 1930s but the rail tankers were discharged in the sidings into a pipeline which passed under the Bude line.
(Wessex collection)

SOUTHERN RAILWAY (S.7)
Holsworthy
The holder is prohibited from entering the Companies' Trains Not Transferable
Admit **One** to Platform 1d.
AVAILABLE ONE HOUR
This Ticket must be given up on leaving Platform.
**FOR CONDITIONS SEE BACK.**
4659

89. Reflecting the station's former importance in the distribution of fertilisers and feeds, the building was acquired by a local trader in these commodities. Apart from the loss of most of its chimneys, little had changed. In 1994, the windows were boarded up and the site awaited redevelopment. (C.Hall)

88. DMUs came into regular use on 4th January 1965 but this is probably a trial trip prior to that date. Single cars were often operated on the the Bude branch.
(Wessex collection)

90. As the line descends out of the station at 1 in 132 it passes over the 176yd long Derrington Viaduct which crosses the small River Deer. By 1898 concrete had come into favour for civil engineering, but, unlike most structures which were poured on site, this was built from pre-cast blocks. (C.Hall)

# WHITSTONE AND BRIDGERULE

91. The station was not complete when the line opened to Bude and so intending passengers had to wait until 1st November 1898. The standard LSWR designs of the era were used. Note concrete sleepers and new ballast on the down line, probably recorded in the 1950s. (Lens of Sutton)

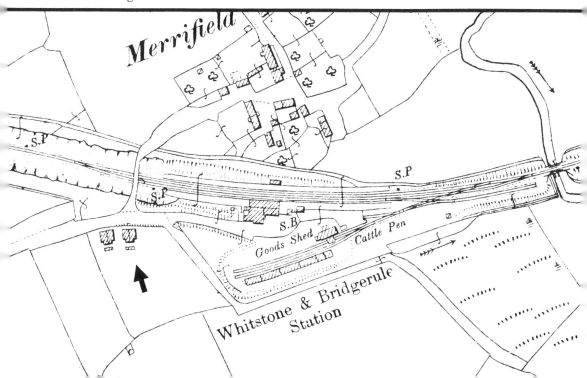

92. N class 2-6-0 no. 1875 waits with a down freight on 3rd July 1948, while Army huts are dismantled in the background. The camp had been served by a trailing siding, the points for which had been in front of the signal box. It branched into two within the camp boundary and was in use from 8th August 1943 until 2nd March 1947 carrying ammunition for the U.S.Army. (J.H.Aston)

93. The loop would accommodate 35 wagons, seldom required except during World War II. N class no. 31841 clatters in with an up freight on 16th July 1957. The yard was shunted by down trains after the connection to the up line was removed in 1931. (Pamlin Prints)

94. The 4.24pm Okehampton to Bude runs past the sidings on 10th June 1960, the rear coach being by the permanent way hut. The popularity of the N class is evident in these pages but only one has been preserved - no. 1874 on the Mid-Hants Railway. (S.C.Nash)

95. While some will gaze at class 3 2-6-2T no. 82025, others will observe that the down platform has two different levels. A 50yd length of platform was removed during WWII. The replacement section was built with "harps & slabs" to the new standard height.
(C.L.Caddy coll.)

| Whitstone | 1928 | 1936 |
|---|---|---|
| No. of passenger tickets issued | 7136 | 4979 |
| No. of season tickets issued | 2 | - |
| No. of tickets collected | 7675 | 5231 |
| No. of telegrams | 554 | - |
| Parcels forwarded | 1465 | 850 |
| Parcels received | 1850 | 2117 |
| Horses forwarded | 7 | 10 |
| Milk forwarded - cans 1928/gallons 1936 | - | - |
| Milk received - cans 1928/gallons 1936 | - | - |
| General goods forwarded (tons) | 412 | 227 |
| General goods received (tons) | 1370 | 2887 |
| Coal, Coke etc. received (tons) | 1618 | 1193 |
| Other minerals forwarded (tons) | 2192 | 291 |
| Other minerals received (tons) | 3219 | 1885 |
| Trucks livestock forwarded | 77 | 157 |
| Trucks livestock received | 10 | 3 |
| Lavatory pennies | - | - |

96. The signal box had 20 levers of which five
were spare and probably used for the wartime
connection. The 30cwt. goods crane is
partially obscured by agricultural equipment
in this July 1963 photograph. (E.W.Fry)

97. One of the two sidings had once run under a roof supported by the two projecting timbers and had passed a single cattle pen on the right. Goods traffic came to an end on 5th September 1964. Passenger traffic was always slight as the population of Bridgerule was about 400 throughout the life of the line. This shed and the main building, together with the platform canopy, were extant in 1994. (C.Hall)

98. The up starter was recorded in June 1966 from a DMU on the 30-chain curve, one of a dozen reverse curves that follow on the three mile descent at 1 in 73. Beyond the bridge, the line passed Glubb's Brickworks siding and entered Cornwall. (Unknown)

# BUDE

99. The station opened to traffic on 10th August 1898 and was soon featured on a postcard. The largest sign bears the words REFRESHMENTS, a welcome sign indeed for a traveller from London in those days. (Lens of Sutton)

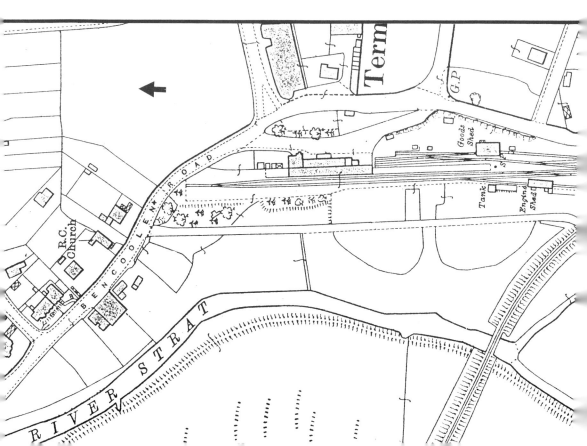

100. The population was about 200 before the railway arrived but the town of Stratton only one mile away was of much greater impor- tance. Many would have hired road transport to reach it. (Lens of Sutton)

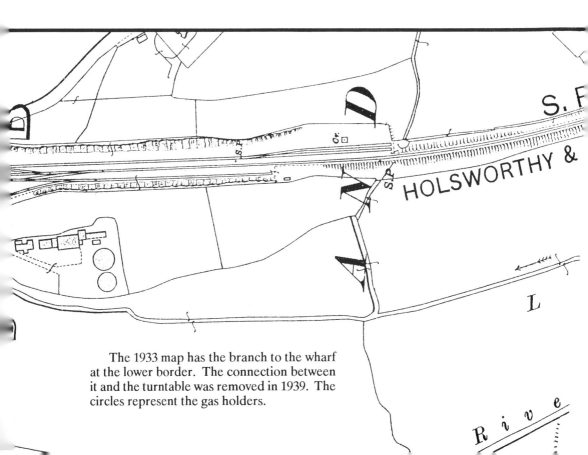

The 1933 map has the branch to the wharf at the lower border. The connection between it and the turntable was removed in 1939. The circles represent the gas holders.

| Bude | 1928 | 1936 |
|---|---|---|
| No. of passenger tickets issued | 16159 | 8923 |
| No. of season tickets issued | 34 | 104 |
| No. of tickets collected | 37710 | 26157 |
| No. of telegrams | 1813 | 3230 |
| Parcels forwarded | 5950 | 4831 |
| Parcels received | 26669 | 31539 |
| Horses forwarded | 54 | 26 |
| Milk forwarded - cans 1928/gallons 1936 | - | - |
| Milk received - cans 1928/gallons 1936 | - | 212 |
| General goods forwarded (tons) | 1106 | 945 |
| General goods received (tons) | 7605 | 9443 |
| Coal, Coke etc. received (tons) | 7154 | 8554 |
| Other minerals forwarded (tons) | 4251 | 1909 |
| Other minerals received (tons) | 4831 | 3429 |
| Trucks livestock forwarded | 178 | 350 |
| Trucks livestock received | 20 | 1 |
| Lavatory pennies | 3306 | 2638 |

101. Class 02 0-4-4T no. 211 was working the 7.55am to Halwill when recorded on 16th July 1906. This class appeared in the area in 1905 but was largely displaced by the T1s around 1910. This locomotive was later moved to the Isle of Wight where it ran as no. 20 *Shanklin* until 1966. (Lens of Sutton)

102. Upon the outbreak of war, in 1939, many children were evacuated from London and other areas of high risk. A train is discharging evacuees while residents look at this unusual spectacle. The SR produced special trains at short notice many times in the years that followed - see *War on the Line*, the SR's official history, reprinted by Middleton Press. (Lens of Sutton)

103. A horse box was rare in this district when compared with cattle wagons. Very superior, they were fitted with a groom's compartment and vacuum brakes for running in passenger trains. The locomotive is no. E35 of class M7, a type that worked in the area from 1926 to 1952. (Lens of Sutton)

1926

104. The siding on the right was added in May 1939 to cope with holiday traffic but it would have been of value for wartime traffic also. The black box houses a water tap to which a hose is attached for replenishing lavatory tanks in the coaches. (A.F.E.Field)

105. The exterior still carried SR signs when photographed eight years after the company had ceased to exist. Austins of pre-war and post-war designs are also featured. Soon after the line opened, Bude had about 800 residents and nearby Stratton around 1000. By 1951 the total was 5224, this figure nearly doubling in the holiday season. (H.C.Casserley)

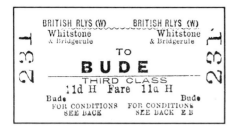

106. Seen from left to right in September 1956 are the starting signals, the abattoir, the up siding, the main line, wagons by the coal chute for the gasworks, the 32-lever signal box and the locomotive shed, ash pit and coal dock. (H.C.Casserley)

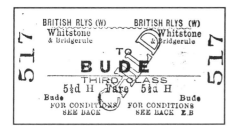

BRITISH RLYS (W)    BRITISH RLYS (W)
Whitstone           Whitstone
& Bridgerule        & Bridgerule
          TO
       **BUDE**
       THIRD CLASS
    5½d H  Fare  5½d H
Bude                    Bude
FOR CONDITIONS   FOR CONDITIONS
  SEE BACK        SEE BACK  E.B

517    517

2nd · SINGLE    SINGLE · 2nd
    Dunsland Cross  to
Dunsland Cross    Dunsland Cross
Bude                    Bude
      **B U D E**
  (S)   3/0   FARE  3/0   (S)
For conditions see over  For conditions see over

4979    4979

107. The 1.55pm to Okehampton stands at the well kept station on 25th May 1957 when it still had a refreshment sign. Class 3 2-6-2T no 82017 would take the three coaches as far as Halwill where they would be attached to the 12.58 Padstow to Waterloo. Arrival in London was due at 8.25pm. A shunter's pole leans against the van. (T.Wright)

108. Class T9 is ready to work the 3.17pm to Okehampton on 7th June 1960. The vans on the right would form the "7pm mails" which carried large quantities of dead rabbits until they were decimated by myxamatosis in 1954. (S.C.Nash)

109. There appears to be a step down from the 50ft turntable to the shed road. The concrete fence on the left served as a means of reducing the nuisance of wind borne ash. The locomotive is class T9 no. 30718 and is seen on 7th June 1960. (S.C.Nash)

110. The guard wanders across the track with a broom as class 3 no. 82023 reverses onto two coaches and two vans on 16th June 1962. Judging by the length of the shadows, it is the last train of the day - the 7.2pm to Halwill. The main platform could take ten coaches. (R.C.Riley)

111. The starting signals had been moved 38yds nearer to the signal box in 1939, thus allowing longer trains to be accommodated. Ten coach trains at peak holiday times became more normal and troop trains of 16 vehicles were seen on many occasions. Two sufficed for the 5.32pm to Halwill with no. 31889 on 8th July 1963. The 5.28 arrival from Okehampton is in the background. (T.Wright)

112. Despite pleading insufficient funds to take the line to Stratton, the LSWR found enough money to embellish its terminus with stone quoins, a lavish gable and an ornate finial on the porch of the station master's garden door. (E.W.Fry)

113. The booking hall was provided with a dormer window to improve illumination and the gentlemen's area was given very generous ventilation. The local authorities failed to recognise that the coming of the railway was the most important single event in the development of the town and allowed rapid demolition of this significant monument. Dwellings now occupy the site. (J.H.Aston)

114. Palms once grew on the left, before the siding was laid, impressing on the crowds of arriving holidaymakers that they had reached a mild climate. Class 4 2-6-4T no. 80037 waits at platform 1 with the penultimate train of the day on 17th July 1964, the 5.35. (R.Palmer)

115. Platform 2 was occupied by the 9.40am to Halwill on 27th July 1964 but the end loading dock had seen little use in recent years. The steam depot closed on 7th September following and four pairs of enginemen, the cleaner and the night shedman then became redundant - sacked in contemporary language. Servicing facilities were retained until January 1965. (J.H.Aston)

117. The water tank was roofless and the sheds deserted in the brief DMU era. A single car was detached from others at Halwill to bring in the morning newspapers but two-car sets could be seen during the day. (Lens of Sutton)

116. Class N no. 31855 departs on 28th August 1964, only days before the end of freight traffic on 5th September. No longer would residents listen to the clatter of shunting coal, cattle, building materials and all the other commodities of everyday life which the railway once carried. (C.L.Caddy coll.)

118. Long shadows feature in our last look at Bude. The final train departed on the dark and rainy evening of Saturday 1st October 1966 and was therefore not photographed. Locomotives on the last day of steam (2nd January 1965) included class 4 2-6-4T no. 82040 and class 4 4-6-0 no. 72025 which had to run tender first from Bude. (Lens of Sutton)

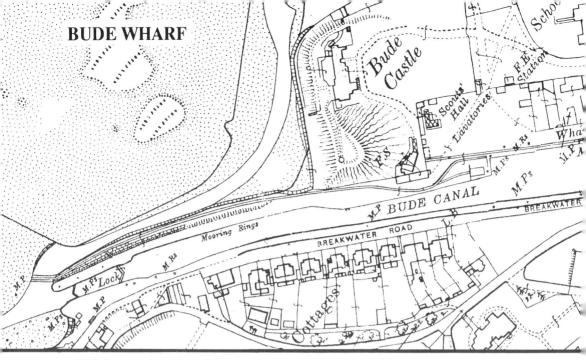

# BUDE WHARF

*(map labels:)* Bude Castle · Scouts' Hall · Lavatories · F.B. Station · Scho... · Wha... · BUDE CANAL · BREAKWATER · Mooring Rings · BREAKWATER ROAD · Lock · Cottages · M.P · M.Ps · M.P.

This is a continuation of the previous map and includes the 4ft. gauge sand carrying plateway (between the words "Lock" and *"BUDE CANAL"*), in use from 1823 to 1923. It was relaid to 2ft gauge and operated from 1924 until 1942, horses providing the power. Sand was tipped into standard gauge wagons and taken inland for land dressing, waterworks filter beds and golf courses. The short siding was removed in about 1933 and the line was shortened in 1940.

119. Class N no. 31844 propels a van towards the wharf on 18th July 1963. The line was about half a mile long and had proved useful for stock storage when Bude station was congested. The remaining part of the Bude Canal and the sea lock were still usable in 1994. (T.Wright)

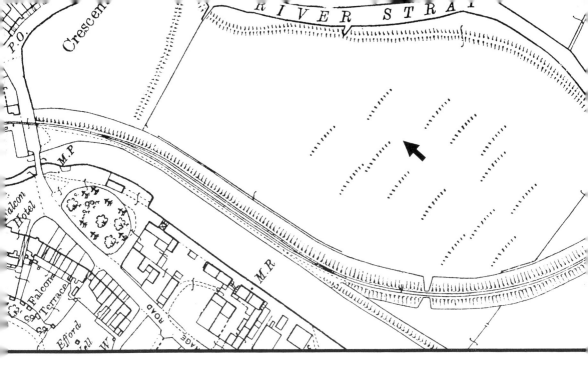

120. Another photograph from 1963, but this one giving the false impression that there was transfer traffic between sea and rail. There was very little, most traffic being coal, fertilisers and feeds to waterside merchants. The line was closed with the end of freight at Bude in September 1964 and the Cornish railway scene lost another byway of charm. (E.W.Fry)